THE 56 SMALL BUSINESS RULES

Best Small Business Adviser

Second Edition

SAMIR HANNA SAFAR

CTAI ACADEMY | SAN DIEGO, CALIFORNIA

This publication provides the Author's opinion in regards to the subject matter contained herein. Neither the Publisher nor the author (Samir Hanna Safer) intends, with this publication, to render legal, accounting or other professional advice.

With regards to licensing of a business enterprise or any other legal, accounting or tax matters, the Publisher and Author strongly suggest that the reader seek, when necessary, the services of appropriate licensed professionals and comply with the local licensing requirements of the community in which the reader resides, or conducts business.

The Publisher and Author disclaims any personal liability, loss or risk incurred as a consequence of the use and application, either directly or indirectly, of any advice, information or methods presented herein.

TABLE OF CONTENTS

"Recovering From Failure Is Often Easier Than Building From Success."

Michael D. Eisner

THE STARTUP

WHAT TO DO AND WHAT NOT TO DO WHEN STARTING YOUR NEW BUSINESS!

1

DO THINK BIG!

"IF YOU WANT TO BE BIG COMPANY TOMORROW, YOU HAVE TO START ACTING LIKE ONE TODAY."

Thomas J. Watson, Jr., IBM

No matter what type of business you're in, the key is to think big to achieve more. Determine how big you want to be, then devise a plan on how you'll achieve that goal. The success of your business depends on your goals. If you're in business, you <u>must</u> have goals. Not only for your business, but your personal finances as well. If you plan for a small business to remain small, it will. Include in your business plan what you offer your customers that none of your existing or future competitor's do. If that's clear in your mind, you don't need to worry about the industry giants moving in next to you...because someday, if you've planned well...you will be that giant!

WHY IS THAT?

I opened a very professional looking and operating copy store in California. Many of my customers asked me if the store was part of a franchise. They were surprised to learn it was not. The point is, I was satisfied with the amount of customers I had, the money I was making and made no plans for expansion. I didn't want the hassle. But guess what happened? Mr. Big, *Staples Office Supplies* opened a store half a mile or so away from me. I was not ready for it, I had not planned for it. I didn't know how to compete with it.

I ended up closing my shop in less than a year. In the meantime, *Mailbox, Etc.* and *Sir Speedy* survived, because not only did they have big dreams, but they had a well thought-out plan on how to make their dreams a reality....step by step.

MORAL:

If you want to last more than five years, you must think big, and plan how you are going to reach that goal.

BELIEVE AND YOU WILL ACHIEVE!

2

DO BE POSITIVE

"I AM AN OPTIMIST. IT DOES NOT SEEM TOO MUCH USE BEING ANYTHING ELSE."

Michel de Montaigne

Attitude, attitude, attitude! The key to being successful in business is how you handle your inner "self-talk". If you're going to start a business, or for that matter, any project in life, you must remember not everything is going to go according to plan. If a door slams in your face, you must believe another door of opportunity will open. You must look for it. Do not give up! You have to be positive! Before I start a company, I always tell myself not to give up. I continually try things. If they don't work, then I try something

else.

The point is I have a goal of making big money, I know I will, and therefore, I don't give up trying to achieve my goal. If you're currently in business and feel like giving up because of all the problems facing you, change your attitude. You need to be open-minded and willing to try things to fix the problem. How else will the problem be solved? It's natural to be a little discouraged, but true entrepreneurs are continually trying to better their businesses, find easier ways to do things, while looking for more ways to make additional money. If you just sit there, hoping the business will take care of itself, you are definitely waiting for a disaster to happen.

WHY IS THAT?

My husband did not like her business. He was always negative, sad, and eventually lost all enjoyment from his work. She did not believe it was worth the effort. If you don't think you can overcome the negativity that comes with every business, you're better off working for somebody else.

MORAL:

If you don't believe your business will be successful, no one else will either!

KEEP YOUR CHIN UP!

3

DON'T ASSOCIATE WITH NEGATIVE-MINDED PEOPLE

"YOUR ATTITUDE, NOT YOUR APTITUDE, WILL DETERMINE YOUR ALTITUDE."

Zig Ziglar

When starting a business, you need lots of positive energy. This positive energy must come from within you. However, if you associate with negative-minded people, that energy will soon be sucked right out of you. It is that simple.

You are ready to start a business when you are excited and energized by an idea that you want to pursue. It's natural that you want to share your excitement, but be aware of who you share your excitement with! Just remember that 90% of the population will tell you why your idea won't work. As an entrepreneur, it's imperative that you beware of this.

When your idea is in this infant stage, you need to STAY AWAY from negative people. The majority of the population are followers who crave routine, security, and avoid taking risks. They may even feel threatened by or jealous of creative people who have big dreams, ideas, and the guts to follow through on them. As Nike advertises, "Just Do It!" Don't give negative nah-sayers the opportunity to deflate your dreams.

WHY IS THAT?

Nine out of 10 days, my husband is depressed about life. I love him dearly and want to spend the rest of my life with him.   However, the last thing I need when I've had a bad day, is to come home and discuss it with him. HE never gives me words of encouragement. So I've learned to listen to my positive "self-talk" to give me the energy and excitement to continue on.

MORAL:
Success breeds success.

JOIN ENTREPRENEUR CLUBS TO ASSOCIATE WITH LIKE-MINDED, POSITIVE-THINKING PEOPLE!

4

DO GET INTO A BUSINESS YOU LIKE AND ENJOY

"TO HAVE WHAT YOU DO AND FEEL THAT IT MATTERS, HOW ANYTHING COULD BE MORE FUN."

Katharine Graham, Washington Post

Another key to success is to be in a business you love! Most rewarding of all is when you can turn your much-loved

hobby into a successful business. Then the work involved in running the business brings you happiness...not headaches! If you truly enjoy and love what you do, that is what will give you satisfaction and success. In fact, you won't even view it as work, but as pure enjoyment! The long hours you devout to building your business will be a pleasure, not a necessary evil. Your long-term success depends on how

*much you enjoy what you do. If you're in it strictly for the money...sad case!
You won't be happy and will not succeed as quickly or easily if you pursue
something you enjoy!*

WHY IS THAT?

My wife is an excellent dentist who knows how to deal with her patients. Her patients
trust her and continue to return to her year after year. However, my wife doesn't enjoy
her practice any longer. She strongly dislikes any confrontations among the office staff
as well as the day-to-day small business management that's necessary when having
your own practice. Even though her employees like her, my wife's lack of enthusiasm
has had a big impact on the performance at the office. As a result, the productivity of
her office staff has fallen and the office has suffered financially. After all that education
and student loans she accumulated. She gave her profession.

MORAL:

*It is important that you love what you are doing in order to take care of the day-to-
day operations.*

DO WHAT YOU LOVE....
THE MONEY WILL FOLLOW!

5

DON'T GET INTO A BUSINESS YOU HAVE NO KNOWLEDGE ABOUT

"THE LESS YOU KNOW HOW TO DO YOUR WORK THE HARDER IST IS TO DO IT."

Henry L. Dohertyt

Your complete overall understanding of the business you chose to run is the key to success or failure. Understand the product, service, or what's involved in the manufacturing before you choose the business. Understand all that's involved in keeping the business going...including the day-to-day operations. Don't rely totally on people you hire for the knowledge. The bottom line is it's your business. No matter how hard an employee works or how much knowledge that person brings to your business, that person will never invest the energy, love, or sweat into the business the way you will to see it become successful. It's your baby, not theirs. Therefore, don't rely totally upon others for a knowledge of the business.

WHY IS THAT?

When I opened my copy store, I had no knowledge of the copy or printing business. I thought I'd just hire people with experience and rely on them to do the business. I found out that it is too expensive to start a business this way on a limited budget. It took me over a year to understand the business and what the customers expected.

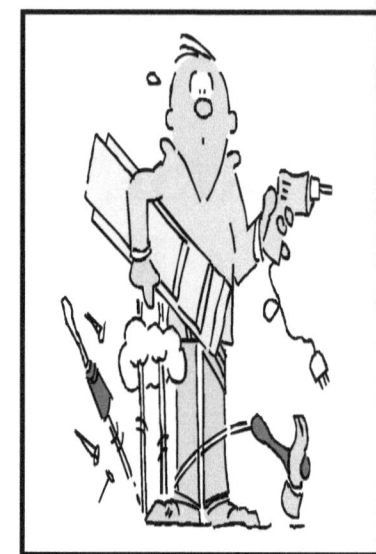

MORAL:

The first step in setting up a successful business is choosing a business you know about.

KNOW YOUR BUSINESS!

6

DON'T START FROM SCRATCH

Oh, it is so painful. For some people, this concept is very hard to grasp. They believe if they're going to start a new business, they have to start from scratch. Not true! Of course, it depends on what kind of business you are starting. It is a challenge and you probably love challenges, because all entrepreneurs naturally do. But wouldn't it be nice to take on some other business that already went through its infancy, worked out the kinks and now is available for an entrepreneur to build on it and modify it to make it even more successful? You should now about some of Microsoft products! Be smart and reduce your losses. It is hard, it can be lonely and your may spend some scary nights wide awake when you're starting a business. All successful entrepreneurs experience this when they first begin. However, don't let that fear paralyze you. It just did not work.

WHY IS THAT?

When I finished one of my inventions, I decided to manufacture it myself. I thought that way I could keep all the profit to myself and keep control of everything. Why should I let people benefit from my invention? So I did the purchasing, I set up the tools, the drills, and so on. I started it all from scratch. Did I keep all the profit to myself from starting from scratch? NO! Suppliers still profited from my invention because I needed to buy the row material from somebody. Was the quality of the product better because I did it all myself? NO! I became overworked and the quality suffered as I tried to meet deadlines.

MORAL:

The reason you are in business is to make money, not work yourself to death!

DON'T REINVENT THE WHEEL!

7

DO BUY AN ESTABLISHED BUSINESS

If you are not starting something completely and uniquely new, then save your soul, money, and nerves! Buy an established business. If you want to open a dry cleaning business or a pizza shop, look around and see if any are for sale in your area. I guarantee you there are lots listed in your local paper. Save yourself the headache of starting from scratch, having to find a building, equipment, employees, etc. Buy smartly. Choose a business you're interested in, a business you understand, a business that's proven successful in the past, and a business you can visualize growing. Research your market. Then buy only what you can afford!

WHY IS THAT?

If you have money available to start a business, you're wiser to invest it in an existing business that has already proven successful. Your investment will not be near as risky and you'll see a return on your investment sooner. Starting a business from scratch can take several months or years before it turns a profit. When you buy an existing business, the profits come a lot faster. In the long run, you get to do what you like best, making money faster. There are always businesses for sale. People get ill, people retire, people want to relocate, people burn out. Look in your local newspaper, business journal or contact a business broker to obtain a listing of businesses for sale near you.

MORAL:

Buy an existing business to get a quicker return on your investment!

BUY A BUSINESS ON ITS WAY UP...NOT DOWN!

8

DON'T BUY A LOSING COMPANY

So you don't want to start from scratch and called a business broker and/or looked in the paper at the businesses for sale. You're wise! Just remember this: People sell their business for a reason. You MUST know what that reason is. Why are they selling? Ask them directly. Check their accounting books, their bank statements, talk with the employees, work in that business for a month or so and be at the business and take notes. Study the business for at least sixty days. Make sure whatever the reason is they are selling, that it is not because the business is in the RED (losing money). Also, do your own investigative work. You can ask your accountant to help you, but don't depend on him/her 100%. You need to make this decision, not your accountant or your broker. You've got more vested. If you are considering buying a company in the RED because it is cheap and you believe you can turn it around and start making profit from it....You must be out of your mind! Run, don't walk, away from it!

Invest your money now and start making a profit sooner by purchasing a sound business. There are plenty of good (in the black) businesses out there that are being sold due to the owner's poor health, retirement, divorce, lack of enthusiasm, or relocation.

WHY IS THAT?

A friend of mine owns a small grocery store that retails to a in a not to exciting area of the city. I asked him one day if he would sell his business. He replied with "Why? I'm making good money."   Business owners who are making money, enjoying the business, and are in good health, will hang on to their businesses. It's their golden egg.

MORAL:

Know what you're buying before you hand out the cash.

RESEARCH BUSINESSES FOR SALE

9

DON'T JOIN A FRANCHISE

"FREE ENTERPRISE WILL WORK IF YOU WILL."

Ray Kroc

Franchising, the true American mall builder. If you have money to invest and are interested in the retail or service sector, buying into a franchise can be an ideal way.....but be careful! Don't join a franchise before you do your homework. There are lots of deceiving franchisers and they are only after the quick bucks. Know how much return you are going to get on your investment and for how long. Know how much support you'll receive from the franchiser, what protection you are given, how other members are doing, and how much free rein you will be allowed. Being a franchisee is not being an entrepreneur. You report to others, what you spend on certain things (advertising, for example) is dictated by the franchiser. You work hard, long hours, and must hand over some of your profits over to the franchiser. Know how much you, as a franchisee, will be getting from the profits.

WHY IS THAT?

Not too long ago I spoke with a submarine sandwich shop franchisee.   He informed me that after everybody, meaning the franchiser, the suppliers, etc.; he ended up with one-eighth of the sub sandwich sales price. He was crying that it was not worth the effort. He could have invested in a non-franchise business and made more money with a lot less headache and hard work.

MORAL:

Don't pay someone else a big share for your hard work.

DO YOUR HOMEWORK!

10

DON'T GET INTO RETAIL IF YOU DON'T LIKE DEALING WITH PEOPLE

"IF YOU DON'T GENUINELY LIKE YOUR CUSTOMERS, THE CHANCES ARE THEY WON'T BUY."

Thomas J. Watson, Jr., IBM

Retail sales is the most difficult type of business the entrepreneur can get into. A retailer must have a special personality and be a true risk taker. Retail means you have to interact directly with the public. You must be a people person who loves dealing with plenty of different people all the time. The most successful retailers are those people who have no problem striking up conversations with complete strangers; who take rejection well; who thrive in a busy, confusing environment; and prefer to be surrounded by people.

WHY IS THAT?

Several studies have been done to determine why some people excel more in one business than another. From these studies it's been found the most successful retail owners possess the following:

- Ability to establish and maintain warm and genuine interpersonal relationships with others (customers);

- Ability to improve other's quality of life (customer satisfaction);

- Ability to learn and master skills before using them (knowing their business thoroughly);

- Ability to work with many people to reach a harmonious goal (little or no conflict) while maintaining control;

- Ability to use effective procedures and make decisions; and

- Ability to organize the work of those around them to ensure things run smoothly and efficiently.

If this describes you, then retail business may be for you!

MORAL:

Use your individual talents to make the most out of your business.

STAY OUT OF RETAIL... UNLESS YOU HAVE THE RIGHT PERSONALITY!

11

DO BELIEVE IN YOUR PRODUCT

I've created a few inventions and have spent lots of money on developing them. Some inventions I stopped at a prototype; others went into production. I failed with most of these inventions because of one factor believing in my product. To me believing in a product as a business person mean selling it.

WHY IS THAT?

After a few months of marketing my product, I stopped believing in it. I loved inventing, but I did not have a strong enough believe in the products to work hard on marketing them to become successful, even though most of my acquaintances thought they were great ideas. If I believed in my product I could of convinced people to buy it by explaining the advantage of that product.

.

MORAL:

Plan ahead...is this product something you'll continue to believe in long after its creation?

NECESSITY IS THE MOTHER OF INVENTION!

12

DO HAVE A SHORT-TERM AND LONG-TERM BUSINESS PLAN

"PEOPLE WHO FAIL TO PLAN, HAVE PLANNED TO FAIL."

George Howell

Having a plan, short and long business plan, whether professionally prepared or prepared on a restaurant napkin, gives lots of confidence and turns nebulous ideas and plans into concrete goals.

Whether you are inventing a new product, marketing a new product or opening a new flower shop, your main objective is to make money. When things are not going right, go back to your plan, and if you're a true entrepreneur, you will say "Aha! This is where I need to make the adjustment". A good business plan that includes both short and long term goals helps you to stay on course. There are no guarantees, of course, but when your venture is successful, you know why. Plus, it's fun to have something to show your peers and say "See, I planned this whole operation...on a restaurant napkin!"

WHY IS THAT?

Whether I'm tired and relaxing on my recliner chair (it's worth noting that my recliner is comfortable leather. Which gets softer as I get older) or energetically pursuing my dreams, the comfort I receive from having a business plan that keeps me on track towards my goal is invaluable.

MORAL:

Have a clear idea of where you are going and then you won't get lost It is easy to get off track.

PLAN YOUR WORK, WORK YOUR PLAN!

13

DO SECURE YOUR IDEA

Whether you have a business, book, or a new invention idea in your head, you must secure it. New and unique ideas that make lots of money are very hard to come by. How many times have you seen products in the stores and said to yourself, "I thought of that ten years ago"?

Ideas are what make us human, make our businesses progress and make us money. Case in point: Did you know the person who invented the ball pen never patented it and never mad a penny off of it.

WHY IS THAT?

If you have an idea and are a serious businessperson, the first thing I suggest you do is register it. There are many ways to do this. One way is to contact the Patent Office at the

Register of Copyrights at the Library of Congress in Washington, DC. You can request free information about filing a patent and registering your idea by calling 1-202-287-9100. However, acquiring a patent can be a very expensive and long, drawn-out process, running into thousands of dollars. An alternative, less expensive way to secure ideas that I use is this: When I get a new idea, I write it down or illustrate it, then have one or two people I know <u>well</u> sign and witness. And date it. I then mail this to myself, by <u>registered</u> mail. I never open the envelope after that. You never know when you'll need to open it... in front of a judge. In my opinion, ideas are as good as the money they produce for you. Just ask my wife, who always says, if it's such a great idea, how come you're not making money from it?

MORAL:

We all have great ideas every now and then. It's only those few who claim and act upon their ideas who find great success.

REGISTER YOUR IDEAS...
BEFORE SOMEONE ELSE HAS THE SAME IDEA...
AND BECOMES A MILLIONAIR!

14

DO INCORPORATE

I know that you must be an entrepreneur...you took the risk in buying this valuable manual! My advice here is very simple. If you have to sign any contract or lease or borrow money, do one thing before that....INCORPORATE. You will value its protection in the future, when and if things turn sour. And the best way to incorporate is to spend the extra money now to hire an attorney to do it right. Or if you are in the least bit legal savvy, you can purchase an "incorporation kit" from any of the larger office supply stores. These kits include step-by-step instructions on how to incorporate and all the forms you will need to do so. This kit runs between twenty-five and seventy-five dollars. Then, of course, there will be filing fees of roughly seventy-five dollars for filing the incorporation forms at the courthouse. It's an easy procedure if you feel confident doing it yourself.

WHY IS THAT?

Before I opened my copy business, my ex-accountant advised me to incorporate. You know what I did? I fired her! Two years later, I had to file bankruptcy and I lost much more than the attorney fees.

Special Note: If something should go sour, should your company ever be sued, should your business lose, should you be ordered to pay, should there not be enough funds, which forces your company to file bankruptcy; the other parties can NOT come after your personal property *if* you are incorporated. On the other hand, if you are NOT incorporated, you can lose everything: your business, your home, your car, even your purebred dog!

MORAL:

Whether you hire an attorney or do it yourself, just incorporate!

INCORPORATE, INCORPORATE, AND INCORPORATE. DID I SAY THAT ENOUGH? OKAY, INCORPORATE!

15

DON'T INVEST YOUR OWN MONEY

"I HAVE ENOUGH MONEY TO LAST ME THE REST MY LIFE, UNLESS I BUY SOMETHING"

Jackie Mason

Anyone who is going to lend you money, wants to see you invest some of yours in the business...unless, of course, you're Donald Trump! Most of the time it is very hard to get loans. But if you can, do it. Different sources include banks, credit unions, and small business loans from the government. Be careful from loan sharks. After you borrow the money, if the business does not work, you still have a chance to keep your spouse happy and you won't be flat broke. Borrowing money to run a business is not a shame. I believe it is the best way of doing business. You will sleep much better when you have liquated assets somewhere.

NOTE: See Section 14 (Incorporating) and Section 16 (Money from Relatives)

WHY IS THAT?

When your business is not making the income you were hoping for, it is easier to walk to your bank and withdraw money from your account, rather than going through the pain of borrowing money from a financial institution. However, once your money is gone, it's much harder to obtain a loan. You see, if you don't have cash, lenders have no collateral, no insurance for the loan. I always tell my banker the slogan "you need money to borrow money". She throws back her head and laughs, then replies, "We are in the business of making money, too!"

MORAL:

It takes money to make money, but borrow the money rather than spend your own. Before yours is all gone!

KEEP YOUR MONEY IN THE BANK!

16

DON'T BORROW FROM RELATIVES

Whether you are already in business or are about to start one, you have to learn the business of borrowing money. It is part of doing business. One thing most business advisers will tell you is to avoid borrowing from your relatives because it will be difficult for you to deal with them until they've been repaid. Their collection system is not formal. It seems natural to think that your relatives would be more lenient with pay-back terms, so it's easy to put them on the back burner. However, they may not be lenient or you put so much pressure on yourself to pay them back at any cost, you cause yourself unnecessary what I call;

"Relative Money Stress Syndrome".

WHY IS THAT?

I had borrowed five thousand dollars from my brother once to meet payroll. Every time I met him, I felt that he was going to ask for the money I owed him. From all the pressure I put on myself, I decided to write him two checks. Each for twenty-five

Hundred dollars. One was to be cashed right away, the other to hold until I had enough money in the bank, he does not need the cash right now. Well, guess what? After just two weeks, he called and wanted to know when he could cash the second check! I knew very well that he had enough money, but he made me feel like I was going to cheat him. I tried very hard that week to save enough money to pay him back. And believe me, when I did, it was an elephant off my back!

Special Note: Some lenders will ask you to guarantee some loans by personal assets (collateral). If at all possible, don't. Try for a signature loan. Other avenues to pursue include: (1) Small Business Loans, (2) Government Grants, and (3) New Business Incubator Projects. Contact the local Small Business Administration office for details.

MORAL:

Borrow money from outsiders but not loan sharks..

DON'T BORROW MONEY FROM YOUR RELATIVES ...OR FRIENDS!

17

DO HAVE WORKING CAPITAL

Working capital is money you need available after your start-up expenses are paid, payroll, utilities, telephone... Don't spend all your money initially on start-up. You must estimate working capital correctly. Some businesses require at least six to nine months of working capital. You should have an idea how much working capital you'll need from the business plan that you've prepared. (Lending institutions will require a complete business plan when you request a loan.) Working capital it is in my opinion is like rain in drought season. Don't expect to make money the minute you start your business. You should expect more expenses than income.

NOTE: See Sections 12 (Plans), 15 (Own Money), and 16 (Relatives).

WHY IS THAT?

There's nothing worse than to get your business all set up, only to have to borrow funds to complete your first job. It's a vicious cycle that once started is very difficult, if not impossible, to break. This reason alone is why most new businesses fail within their first year!

MORAL:

Adjust your spending of working capital as your business progress.

BORROW ENOUGH MONEY
TO KEEP YOUR BUSINESS GOING

18

DON'T BUY EXPENSIVE EQUIPMENT

If the business you're starting needs some sort of equipment or furniture, shop around first. Deal with reputable dealers, get references from business associates, check out warranties, and compare prices. Beware! You get what you pay for. Also don't buy a Cadillac version when all you need at this time is the Vega (are those still made?). You can always trade-up later when your cash flow has been established. You must use your income wisely when starting your business.

WHY IS THAT?

This scenario between myself and my accountant should justify this point. I got a call from him one day as I was leaving for lunch to ask me what I paid for the small copiers in my shop. As if he didn't know (he could've looked it up--he has all my financial records).). But, instead he calls me up to describe to me the copier he just bought at an auction for four hundred dollars. My accountant just had to rub it in. You see, he thought it was much better and cheaper than the six thousand dollar copiers which I had bought brand new only to have them break down on me repeatedly during the first four months my copy shop was in business. The copy technician kept informing me that all new copiers need adjustment the first few months. That's not exactly what a small business owner wants to hear--especially when he's just opened a new copy shop that depends on the copiers running non-stop without glitches!!!

MORAL:

Shop around and buy good, but reasonably priced, merchandise. It is your money, after all.

SPEND WISELY...

19

DON'T BUY SECONDHAND FROM PEOPLE YOU DON'T TRUST

Trust. What is trust in business? After a bad experience, I believed that all people were sharks and as long as they make a buck, they didn't care how nice you were or, as a matter of fact, how stupid you were. I learned to be distrustful. I learned to think and be careful with whom I made deals or purchased specialty items for my kind of business. Not all secondhand purchasing is bad, if you have some kind of warranty. Warranties have to be backed by solid support. Be careful. Do your homework, check out the company, check the address, drive by the company, ask for names of other satisfied customers...and call them!

WHY IS THAT?

I purchase one used folding machine from a man who claimed to be a dealer of that kind machines. I went against the advice of my staff and my gut instinct. I thought I had found a great deal. The guy gave me a paper stating it was a ninety day warranty from his company. After just a few uses, of course, I started experiencing problems with the folding machine. I called the man. He did not return my calls. His address was a P.O. Box. You can fill in the blanks from what happened there. I was fooled by a con man and his piece of paper. Be careful!

MORAL:

It is better to deal with a reputable company that backs up their products...even if you have to pay more. Be cheap smart!

TRUST YOUR INSTINCTS,
YOU WON'T GO WRONG!

20

DON'T SIGN EXPENSIVE LEASES

If you are going to be in business as long as I've been in it, sooner or later, you are going to sign some sort of lease. Either for office space, equipment or whatever. Do sign a lease according to your business plan. Don't overextend yourself nor assume the future is going to be nice to you all the time. Be logical, and don't let emotion sway you to choose an office...no matter how beautiful it is! You want to make sure you have a "beautiful deal". Be a deal maker and a winner. It is your cash flow that will impress investors and not nice office with a window overlooking the ocean.

NOTE: See Section 12 (Business Plans)

WHY IS THAT?

Signing an expensive lease is like a beautiful bride. The beautiful bride who spends lots of money on her wedding, thinking her handsome husband is worth every cent of it. Unfortunately only a few months later, the fickle man runs away with a richer, or younger, woman. Agree only what you can afford and be careful of those convincing sales people!

MORAL:

Don't overextend yourself! Lease is a legal commitment and you are obligated by its terms.

MAKE DUE WITH WHAT YOU CAN AFFORD!

21

DON'T SIGN LONG-TERM LEASES

Again, be careful here. Sometimes, long term leases look attractive either because of the low payment or the freebies you're going to get for signing the long-term lease. Unless you have solid long-term financial backing for your business, avoid this devil. Only sign a long-term lease after your business is well established. Long-term lease looks good on the lesser financial statement and it is less expensive for them to have long-term leases.

WHY IS THAT?

For one of my businesses, I had an option to sign a five-year lease with the first three months free and lower monthly rent, or sign a month-to-month lease with higher monthly rent. I was so confident that I was going to make it...no matter what.... (That is NOT the attitude you need to take when dealing with legal contracts), that I signed the longer lease. After only one year, the economy started to slide (can I blame President Carter?) and my business was one of the thousands of victims. But I still had to pay the term of the lease because the landlord refused to give me a break. It was a huge loss. So start slow and evaluate your business progress. You can always negotiate when things get on solid ground.

MORAL:

Everything is negotiable except health and death.

START WITH A MONTH-TO-MONTH LEASE

22

DO PAY COD WHEN YOU START

If you are not incorporated. This what I think. Some business people may disagree with me on this, but "net thirty" is like charging things. What I recommend is paying COD when you start your new business for at least the first three months. This will really give you the true feeling of your cash flow. Cash goes out of the door faster than you can imagine. Keep your eyes on your spending. The last thing you want to do is overextend yourself during the first few months in business. You may never be able to overcome it.

WHY IS THAT?

You know, I thank the people who start me on COD, because they know purchasing merchandise without having to pay for it immediately, is like having a Gold card. It's too easy to lose track on how much you are charging. Plus, when the bill comes in, it's too tempting to pay the "minimum balance due"...and the next thing you know, all of your payments are going to interest and your principle barely goes down!

MORAL:

Cash accounting is a simple accounting method. It gives me more actual feeling of my performance the first few months.

CASH- NOW YOU SEE IT, NOW YOU DON'T.

23

DO SELECT A NICE
COLOR LOGO

Image is very important. A logo represents you. The colors of a logo represent your business. Have a professional help you decide upon and design a logo for your company. If you design a logo yourself, ask for other people's opinions. What do they think? What suggestions or ideas can they offer? Your logo is what defines your business forever. Logo should not be just a design but a thought and a message.

WHY IS THAT?

I believe that logos should be simple in design, but unique. Look at the egg. You cannot design a better egg. The same for logos. Consider the most familiar logos: Nike, IBM, or Exxon. They are very simple logos, yet people recognize them instantly. Simplicity is best.

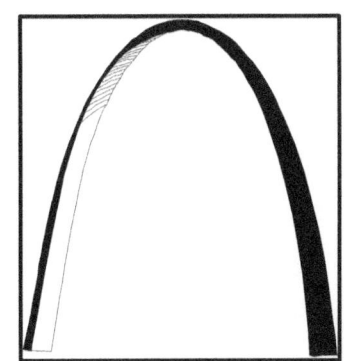

MORAL:

Give it the old kiss routine.....Keep It Simple!

A LOGO IS YOUR COMPANY'S SIGNATURE.
MAKE IT SIMPLE, YET EYE-CATCHING!

"Good Fortune Is What Happen When Opportunity Meets With Preparation."

Thomas Edison

CONDUCTING BUSINESS

WHAT TO DO AND WHAT NOT TO DO WHEN CONDUCTING BUSINESS!

24

DO LOOK CLEAN

"MORE OFTEN THAN NOT, THINKS AND PEOPLE ARE AS TEHY APPEAR."

Malcolm Forbes

Personal hygiene is very important! It may not be fair, but your customers and clients base their first impression of you and your business from your appearance. Therefore, it's imperative that the last thing you do before you leave to start your day is look in a full-length mirror. You NEED to look sharp! Make sure your clothes are straight and fit you well, your hair is neat, your shirt is not stained, etc. Wearing anti-perspiring deodorant is not an option. Body order is murderous to the business person. Also it's imperative that cologne and perfume are not overdone. Believe it or not, that's one of the quickest ways to lose a customer! And men, please make sure your ties are straight, your facial hair is neatly trim (this means nose and ears as well!) The overall look you are trying to achieve is one of neatness. If you need help, pick up one of the many books on dressing for success and study it or contact an image consultant listed in the yellow pages of your local directory.

WHY IS THAT?

People feel more comfortable dealing with clean, well-kept people. If you're sloppy, they may assume your work is sloppy as well. If you are trying to make deals, your success depends on how much respect your counterpart has for you. Even if you are not out on a business call, looking good makes you feel good, helping lift your mood and your outlook on life.

MORAL:

If you want to be successful, you've got to dress the part! Dress for success!

ALWAYS LOOK YOUR BEST WHEN OUT IN PUBLIC!

25

DON'T BECOME A CHEAP EMPLOYEE OR LET THE BUSINESS OWN YOU!

"FEW RICH MEN OWN THEIR OWN PROPERTY. THE PROPERTY OWNS THEM."

Robert Green Ingersoll

What this means is don't work in your business where your average income is less than five dollars an hour. If you start at six in the morning and stay till midnight, i.e., you put in long hours, you're a cheap employee and the business owns you. Don't let yourself get caught in this situation! Always remember that you are in business to make money...and lots of it, not to sacrifice your life. It should be you that manages your business to reach the goal of making it grow while making money and having fun! Concentrate on those objectives, and only those. If you find yourself spending time concentrating on the little things that need to be done, like fixing the drill or copiers, you're becoming a cheap employee. Hire people to do the little non-consequential stuff.

WHY IS THAT?

If you become a cheap employee, I can almost guarantee you that you are going to fail within the first five years. For several reasons, including:

Your business owns you;

2)   Your family life will suffer;

3)   Your social life will suffer;

4)   Your health may begin to suffer;

5)   You are no longer a well-rounded person; and

6)   You will suffer burn-out and close or sell your business due to lack of interest.

MORAL:

All work and no play makes Jill (or Jackal) a dull, sad person.

MANAGE YOUR BUSINESS
DON'T LET THE BUSINESS MANAGE YOU!

26

DO STAY HEALTHY: PHYSICALLY AND MENTALLY

"THE FIRST WEALTH IS HEALTH"

R. W. Emerson

Any entrepreneur who forgets to take care of him/herself is wasting their life, yes their life. What is the use of creating a successful business, earning all the money and having all the successes, when you don't take care of your health and begin to ail? You won't be around to enjoy the fruits of your labor. Don't tell me you are doing for your family or your kids. Success in business life is very short period. Good health means sharp minds. There are exception to this rule of course.

WHY IS THAT?

Good health will help you to stay sharp and alert which gives you the ability to make better deals. So eat right, drink plenty of fluids, certain kind of fluids could be harmful to your business. Get plenty of rest, get outside and exert some physical energy and take your vitamins (on a full stomach for the best results).

MORAL:

Most people will take care of their cars more than their health.

**DO FOR YOUR BODY
WHAT YOU WANT YOUR BODY
TO DO FOR YOU!**

27

DON'T HIRE RELATIVES (OR CLOSE FRIENDS)

The fastest way to ruin a happy family or close friendship is to hire your family or friends to work for you. First of all, they will learn to resent you for telling them what to do. They'll conveniently forget that you own the company, not them. They'll also expect to be treated better than any of your other employees....and be paid better! This is a lose-lose situation.

WHY IS THAT?

A LONG time ago I was employed at my father's company. He had a full staff. Yet he constantly expected better performance from me, because I was his own flesh and blood. He worked me harder and gave me little or no praise for jobs well done. I felt like a slave. Then to go home and continue "being at work"

was the pits. Everyone needs a break. Give yourself a break, hire people not in your circle of family or close friends.

Moral:

Keep your private and business life separate! Just like separating church and state! Is it that simple?

FIND EMPLOYEES THROUGH ACQUAINTANCE REFERRALS OR "COLD ADS" ONLY!

28

DO HIRE PEOPLE WITH NICE SMILES

Did you know that some people make a living teaching job applicants and business executives how to smile to get ahead? They do! That's because a smile, a nice smile that shows sincerity and reaches the eyes, makes people trust you and want to do business with you! Plus a nice smile simply makes you and your customer feel good. Everyone knows how to smile. It's simply a matter of using it! You have to have a nice smile to get and keep your customer's faith in you and the business. When you pick your staff, make sure they have that magical smile. Look at the Disney Characters (some of them). It's that magical smile that brings the customers back!

WHY IS THAT?

When's the last time you bought ice cream or all those other wonderfully fattening delights that are totally against your health requirements? Did the cashier look at you making you feel guilty, with a scowl on her face? Why, of course, not! She smiled that magical smile that lit up her eyes, and made you smile in return. And what happened? You liked her and wanted to come back again and again to buy more ice cream! The smile worked, didn't it?

MORAL:

A smile makes your customers feel appreciated and keeps them coming back.

KEEP ON SMILING!

29

DO HIRE GOOD-LOOKING PEOPLE

Good looking receptionists in any business is an American way. Corporate America has always believed the first impression is a lasting impression. That goes for the receptionists. Dentists always try to have good looking receptionists. Maybe to ease the patient's fear. But I think it helps! It is all image when dealing with businesses. Don't fool yourself into believing otherwise. If you think you don't look good, get some help from image consultants. I'm in no way prejudice against how people look. But the reality is, in business, that is the way it is. I can't change it, and neither can you.

WHY IS THAT?

I had lunch one day with my friend who's a good looking salesman for a large corporation. He was upset because he was not top salesman

of the month. I asked him what happened. He said that his manager hired this new good-looking female and she was making record sales. I told him that is because she's better looking than him. He said that was for sure. Then I told him he needed a haircut. He got the message.

MORAL:

It may not be fair, but life's not fair. Learn from other's experiences. Hiring unattractive people can actually hurt your business!

**FOR ALL POSITIONS
THAT DEAL DIRECTLY WITH THE PUBLIC...
HIRE ATTRACTIVE PEOPLE!**

30

DO HIRE PEOPLE SMARTER THAN YOU

If you think you are the smartest, the wittiest person in your particular business, believe me there is one person out there smarter than you! If you think you are a hurricane, you are going to be beaten by a typhoon. Some executives are afraid to hire people more knowledgeable than they are because they feel threatened and are afraid of losing their positions. Remember, this is your business! It's up to you to hire a smart staff that's willing to give you ideas. Doing so can only help your business progress and become more profitable. The bottom line is you are the one who makes the final decisions, but do it through having good support from people smarter than you.

WHY IS THAT?

When I was managing the entire computer operation for an international company (my young days), I always tried to hire people smarter than me. Between my experience (I had more), and their knowledge backing me up, these people made my job much easier.

Just look at the President of the United States. Thank God, we have smarter people (advisors) that surround him...though not always!   No smart person wants to be President.

MORAL:

urround yourself with smarter people, and you'll

learn even more!

HIRE PEOPLE FOR THEIR KNOWLEDGE, THEN LEARN FROM IT!

31

DO HIRE OUTSIDE SALES PEOPLE

If one of your business goals is to find new customers constantly, then you need a sales force out there knocking on the doors...knocking....knocking....and knocking. You and your sales force have to go out there and find and get the business. Customers need to be reminded of your business consistently. For some reason, customers tend to have very short memories. As a business owner, you need that constant reminder to your customers, to find and keep their business. Outside sale reps to me are like a pipeline between my business and the client.

WHY IS THAT?

Customers tend to have very short memories.   If your sales staff is not continually approaching current and potential customers, other sales reps from other companies will. The result: the customer will give their business to the other company.

MORAL:

Business is no different than anything else. Out of sight, out of mind.

PERSISTENCY PAYS OFF!

32

DO GIVE SOME INCENTIVES TO BOOST MORAL

Incentives are the most effective way to not only boost your employees' morale, but to increase productivity which, in turn, helps you as the business owner, meet your objectives! You'd be surprised at how much effort people will give to earn that extra dollar. I can't explain it. I just know they do it! Over the years, I've seen people work twice as hard for that little extra incentive.

WHY IS THAT?

Since we implemented a $100 to $200 bonus for each employee in the office who produced certain levels of production dollars, we found the production increased by almost thirty-five percent! Amazing. Unfortunately, not everybody appreciates and will work harder for bonuses.

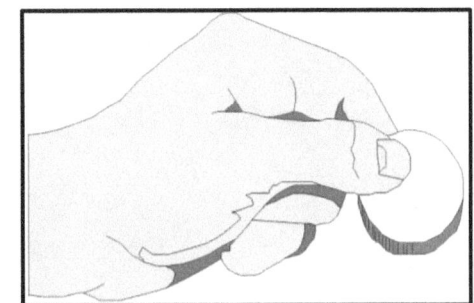

MORAL:

Put a carrot in front of a rabbit and he'll exert the extra effort to obtain it.

INCENTIVES ARE WORTH THEIR WEIGHT IN GOLD.
USE THEM!

33

DO LISTEN TO YOUR EMPLOYEE'S ADVICE

"THERE ARE NO BAD SOLDIERS, ONLY BAD OFFICERS."

Napoleon

If your company has employees, make sure you listen to what they have to say regarding the business. It is wise to have at least one scheduled weekly meeting with your employees to discuss situations that have developed, discover solutions together, and give special recognition to those employees who did an excellent job the week before.

WHY IS THAT?

Listening to your employees, that work with you day in and day out and know your business almost as well as you do, can be a very effective way to solve problems and increase productivity and profits. To me, I find it much cheaper and more effective than hiring an outside consultant who doesn't know my business as well.

MORAL:

Ask for your employees' opinions and suggestions and you will receive them.

LISTEN, LISTEN, LISTEN!

34

DO ADVERTISE

"NO ONE EVER WENT BROKE UNDERESTIMATING THE TASTE OF THE AMERICAN PEOPLE."

H. L. Mencken

You do have a choice! You can advertise your business or you can advertise to go out of business. No matter what kind of business you are in, YOU MUST ADVERTISE your services, products, or ideas if you want to be successful.

Sure, advertising can get expensive, but isn't it a lot more expensive to lose everything you've put into the business? You must advertise! And remember, word of mouth is the best advertising you could ever have. Don't be shy in letting people know about you or about your product or services.

WHY IS THAT?

When I mention in casual conversation that my wife has her own dental practice, I can't begin to count how many times I've heard, "Oh? I'm looking for a new dentist!" Most of the time, I don't have a pen to give them her number, but if I have her business card, I'm sure we added to her new patient list. My wife had the same problem of striking up conversations with strangers when she first began. Talking about one's self just makes some people uncomfortable...but it's necessary as a business owner!

MORAL:

Carry business cards with you at all times. Pass them out at every opportunity that comes along. You must learn to advertise your business....it starts with you.

THE BEST ADVERTISING IS FREE...
WORD-OF-MOUTH!

35

DO HAVE ANNUAL PROMOTIONS AND SALES

"THE FISH SEES THE BAIT, NOT THE HOOK."

Chinese proverb

Don't tell me that you can stay in business for long if you don't consistently promote your business. You can't! Marketing your product or service should never stop. If it does, you will be closing your doors even before that giant competitor arrives. There are so many ways to successfully promote your business. The rule of thumb is to run an ad continually week after week. The purpose is to keep your business's name in front of the consumers (building name awareness in the minds of the consumers). In addition to that you should also plan on having one large promotion per year and no more than four "sales" per year. These events are designed to attract new customers, especially the ones who have just moved into your area. The idea here is growth and making more money!

WHY IS THAT?

If your business is a barbershop, make sure you send out coupons three or four times a year to the residents within a five-mile radius of your shop. In addition, you might hold a "cut-a-thon" as your annual promotion. Invite local media to cover the event, ask celebrities to get their haircuts, and promote that 25% of all proceeds that day will be donated to a charity of your choice. No you won't make more money per haircut, but you will receive a lot of exposure and develop a good name for you within the community. An event like this has great repercussions for a long, long time!

MORAL:

Keep your business's name a familiar one within the community.

BE CREATIVE!
PUT ON UNUSUAL AND UNIQUE PROMOTIONS
THAT THE CONSUMERS WILL REMEMBER!

36

DON'T MANUFACTURE
BEFORE SALES

If you have an idea for a product, service or book.....HOLD ON!! Don't run to put that product into production. Make the sale first. Find a client. Test the market for its reception to your product, service or idea. You should apply this principal whether you are an inventor with a new idea or a manufacturer with some kind of product. It ties up thousands of dollars having inventory gathering dust!

WHY IS THAT?

I was going to have this book written and ready for sale way before I started advertising it. Then I realized that I was going to be spending a lot of money doing that. What if it did not sell? Experience has taught me that it's imperative to find the customer for the product *before* you present the product to the market. The same here. I advertised and the response was overwhelming! That was when I knew <u>for certain</u>, this book was wanted and needed in the marketplace. That's when I decided to make it a reality. Best of all, the book is paying for its own production!

MORAL:

Don't count your chickens before they hatch.

TEST YOUR MARKET PRIOR TO PRODUCTION!

37

DON'T SELL BELOW COST

"A BUSINESS THAT MAKES NOTHING BUT MONEY IS A POOR BUSINESS."

Henry Ford

If you are selling a product or service, and I'm assuming you are or are going to be, you must know your cost. How much will it cost you to have that product ready for sale? Your sales price must be at least three times that amount! Make this one of your principles of running a business.

NOTE: See Section 44 (Customer Satisfaction)

WHY IS THAT?

Sometimes competition makes you want to lower your prices to keep customers. Don't! Instead stress the benefits your customers receive from doing business with you rather than your competition. Remember, if you're

going to sell at cost or below cost, it's better to ask that customer to go and purchase the product from your competition. No need to make that sale. You're not making any money on it, and this way you'll still have the product to sell to someone else at a profit! Besides, if that other company is selling at their cost or below their cost, they are not making any money. No matter how many sales they make, that company will soon be out of business...and then those customers will return to you because you'll still be around!

MORAL:

f you are going to sell at cost or below cost, that is the signal that you will be going out of business soon.

PRICE YOUR PRODUCT CORRECTLY!

38

DO KEEP YOUR EYE ON EXPENSES

Business expenses are a part of doing business. You need to spend money to make money! But watch out and make sure you're not spending it faster than it's coming in. Business expenses need to be specially managed. You must know what your overhead is in order to determine your profit. You don't need an accountant to tell you that. You know it because you are an entrepreneur.

WHY IS THAT?

As the entrepreneur, you should be aware at all times of the status of your expenses. If your money is spent on items not necessary to conduct business, you will soon find yourself in trouble. I know I've said it before, but here it is again: Watch your money! Be careful with every dollar that goes out. It is your money that you worked hard to earn.

MORAL:

If your expenses outweigh your income for too long, find a solution. If you can't, then it's time to do something else.

SPEND YOUR MONEY WISELY!

39

DON'T SPEND YOUR MONEY LAVISHLY

"HE SPENDS MONEY AS IF HE CAN'T STAND TO KEEP ANYTHING THAT HAS ANYBODY ELSE'S PICTURE ON IT."

Jeanne Robertson, humorist

This "Don't" is very simple. If you don't understand what I mean, you are not a business person. You are a kid who got lucky. Some short-term entrepreneurs succeed and quickly make a lot of money, then lose it just as fast. Then they get out before their creditors catch up with them.

WHY IS THAT?

The first thing I noticed about fly-by-night business owners who spent their money (or someone else's money lavishly) is they rent a very expensive, upscale office; fill it with the most expensive

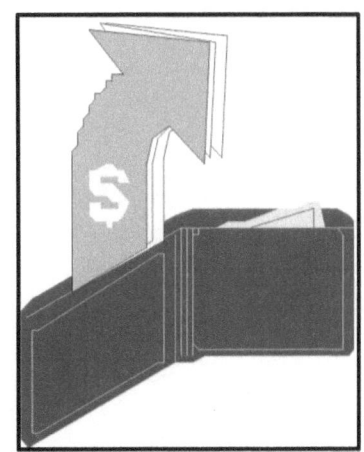

furniture, then hire a gorgeous, and usually, dim-witted receptionist.   After a few months, they were back to bouncing checks. Enough said.

MORAL:

If you're serious about being a truly successful entrepreneur, you will spend your money wisely. Impress people with your product or service, not your office trappings when you are starting out.

IF YOU DON'T HAVE IT, DON'T SPEND IT!

40

DO PAY YOUR TAXES AND KEEP GOOD RECORDS

It is so easy not to pay taxes: Federal income, social security, payroll, and in some instances, state, local, and small business taxes. The government doesn't have a collection person calling you every thirty days to remind you about your overdue bill, like other creditors. So when small business owners get behind in paying bills, the first thing, and I guess the easiest bill, to put on the back burner is the tax bill...right?

Just as important as paying your taxes, is keeping good records. They go hand-in-hand. If you ever get audited by the IRS, it's essential to have support documents to back you up.

WHY IS THAT?

When I created my first invention twenty years ago, I called the Small Business Administration and they offered to give me a free small business start-up consultation.

A few days later, the free advisor, a retired businessman in his sixties, showed up at my door. He told me the best advice he could give me was to pay my taxes. He explained that the other businesses can be dealt with, but when it comes to the IRS, it is a different story. Ten years later, I got into financial trouble. The first thing my attorney wanted to know was if my tax bill was current. It was. He was relieved and said the rest was easy! It was hard on me, but easy on him.

MORAL:

If you're not a great record-keeper, terrible about filing taxes on time, and don't believe the nightmare the IRS can give you, maybe you shouldn't get involved in business.

PAY YOUR TAXES, FIRST!

"Man Who Waits For Roast Duck To Fly Into Mouth Must Wait Very, Very Long Time."

Chinese proverb

THE CUSTOMER

WHAT TO DO AND WHAT NOT TO DO WHEN DEALING WITH THE CUSTOMER.

41

DO KNOW YOUR CUSTOMER TYPE

" YOU WIN CUSTOMERS BY QUALITY RATHER THAN PRICE."

Jean Ridley, retail consultant

What is your target market? Who are your customers? Who do you want to do business with? What type of people would use your product or service? You need to determine your IDEAL Customer so you know who you're dealing with.

What is the sex? Male or Female?

What is the age range? 12-18, 25-54, 25-39, 65+, etc.

Where do they live? In rented apartments or mortgaged homes?

How far are they from your business? Miles? Different Cities? States? Worldwide?

What is the median annual income? $20K, $35K, $100K, +

What is the marital status? Single? Married? Divorced? Widowed?

Are there children in the household? Number? Ages?

You get the picture. There's a lot more questions you can ask yourself about your ideal customer. Use your imagination. The more you know about who you're doing business with, the more successful you'll become in determining what they want, what will satisfy them, and keep them coming to you to do business.

WHY IS THAT?

Before you can begin advertising, before you can determine what your customer's expect, before you can determine what to offer and what not to offer, you need to know your customers. How else can you please them and encourage them to do business with you?

MORAL:

Know what your customers like and don't like.

GET TO KNOW YOUR CUSTOMERS!

42

DO KISS ASS WITH YOUR CUSTOMERS

From time to time you are going to be meeting with some unpleasant clients to make a sale. You ARE going to be nice to them. You ARE going to treat them like they are the most important people on the face of the Earth. Why? Because you want to win them over, get their business and have them refer their acquaintances to you as well.

WHY IS THAT?

You have to think of your customers as your boss. They are in a sense. The customers dictate how much is sold, which determines your profit. Which means to move up the ladder of success as an entrepreneur, you have to kiss ass. It is the low point of doing business, but you can't escape it. You have to be nice all the time to your customers--no matter what. When

you close the deal, you are going to be very satisfied, your profits will rise, and your business will grow since your customers are happy and tell others about you. So, you see, it's worth it in the long run.

MORAL:

Treat others as you would want to be treated.

PUCKER UP!

43

DO LISTEN, LISTEN, LISTEN

"ADVICE IS SELDOM WELCOME, THOSE WHO NEED IT MOST, LIKE IT LEAST"

Samuel Johnson

Just as you should listen to your employee's ideas and suggestions, you should listen to your customers as well. I cannot say it enough! Listen! I envy the people who have this quality. They are able to really listen to their customer's needs, comments, and complaints and turn them into desirable business qualities that make their business even more profitable! Also, listen to your vendors. Always listen first, then negotiate.

WHY IS THAT?

My teacher tried to teach me to be a better listener in kindergarten. I bet yours did the same. But, the teacher never told me how I could make more money if I learned to really listen. So, I didn't listen! I've learned the hard way! Now, I listen to my spouse all the time!

MORAL:

Open your ears and mind to all that everyone shares with you.

LISTING IS AN ART.

44

DO KNOW WHAT YOUR CUSTOMERS EXPECT

All your customers expect one thing: one hundred percent satisfaction. The automakers of America during the 1970's thought if they made a lemon, that it was somehow okay, because customers expected that once in awhile. However, the Japanese were waiting and watching and learning. They decided to give the Americans more than they expected. Give them good service, quality products, and satisfaction guarantees. As you know, the big three American automakers found themselves in serious trouble!

WHY IS THAT?

Your customers expect satisfaction and you've got to respect that. If you receive something from a mail-order catalog and you were expecting more, that catalogue is doomed. This is why photographs are so very helpful in presentations. Although you had an idea of what this manual was about from the sample page you reviewed before purchasing it, I hope this manual is more than what you expected.

MORAL:

Deliver what your customers expect...or more!

KNOW WHAT YOUR CUSTOMERS WANT!

45

DO MAKE CUSTOMER SATISFACTION YOUR NUMBER ONE PRIORITY

The customer is always 1000% right! If you want to make sales and get a good reputation, you must guarantee customer satisfaction. It always works! People feel more comfortable. Plus, people are willing to pay more for that peace of mind. So do account for that cost in your pricing. Another benefit is when a customer is happy with a business, they tell their friends about it, who tell their friends, and so on. Your company then reaps the awards of free advertising! Unfortunately, some people abuse guarantees, but the increase in sales due to this policy is incredible and makes it a must to a successful business. Remember the life blood of any business is its customers. Without them, there is no profit, no work, and no business.

WHY IS THAT?

A customer buying an item or a service who understands that he is not going to be ripped off, will help him to make a quicker buying decision. Although Nordstrom's (retail department store) is expensive, I shop there regularly because their return policy makes me a comfortable customer. If I don't like something after I get home, I know I can exchange it or get my money back with no  questions. I'm willing to pay extra for this peace of mind. As a result, I always shop at Nordstrom's when I need something they carry. On the other hand, I shop at K-Mart who offer guarantees as well. Unfortunately, K-Mart asks questions.

MORAL:

Keep the customers happy and they'll keep coming back for more...plus tell their friends about you, who tell their friends...and their friends...

DELIVER WHAT YOU PROMISE!

46

DO DELIVER MORE THAN CUSTOMERS EXPECT

This is not a new philosophy. If you give people a little more than what they expected, you win them over. As an entrepreneur, this should be one of your prime objectives. Whether you offer a service or product, this objective is something you are going to benefit from. The customer will feel as if he is getting a great deal.

WHY IS THAT?

The cobbler who fixes the broken heal for the "mean lady", then polishes them for her at no additional charge, has just won her over because she was expecting to get the shoes fixed, but not the shine.

MORAL:

Go the extra mile for your customers. Little extras make big differences in customer satisfaction and your profits.

THE CUSTOMER IS ALWAYS THE MOST IMPORTANT ELEMENT OF YOUR BUSINESS... KEEP THEM HAPPY!

47

DO HAVE ON-TIME SERVICE

On-time service. Whether you deliver goods or perform a service, you must provide them by the date you promised. Every time you break that promise, no matter what your excuse, you lose your customer's respect and, possibly, their business! Don't ever use the "flat tire" or any other excuse, for that matter. On-time service tells customers that your business is a professional, well-planned, under-control operation that runs like a well-oiled machine. On-time service produces repeat customers. If your operation can't meet the promised date to your customer, you need to make a full evaluation of the situation, then adjust accordingly. You must let the customer know before the promised date if it won't be met and advice of the new promised date. Don't EVER wait for the customer to come pick up the order and find out it's not ready!

WHY IS THAT?

I bought my wife four gold bracelets for Mother's Day from a jeweler she'd bought from for years. One of the bracelets didn't look as well made as the others. My wife returned it. The jeweler informed her he'd order another one and asked her to come pick it up in two weeks. Because my wife is a very patient person, she agreed to wait. In two weeks she went back to pick up the bracelet. The jeweler hadn't received it yet, and promised he'd have it within a week. This went on and on. What a stupid business man because

my wife loves gold (who doesn't?), but he lost her business, forever.

MORAL:

Don't make a promise you can't keep.

KEEP YOUR PROMISES!

48

DO HAVE QUICK SERVICE

Quick turn-around service. This is another very important objective of business. I hope you've heard this expression before. As I said in an earlier section, the business that gives a little more than what the customer expects, will succeed. Quick turn-around is one of the ways to meet this objective while not sacrificing quality. Whether you are in the fast food, car repair, or publication business, give your customer a "promised by" date (or time), and

then have the order or service completed sooner. The customer will be thrilled!

WHY IS THAT?

People in the United States are always in the fast lane. They want something "now, actually yesterday would have been

better". However, some things just can't be done as fast as you would like them to be. Quality is *always* more important than speed. How many times have you found yourself in a dentist's chair thinking to yourself "I wish he'd hurry up"? The point is, the dentist can't hurry up. If he is to do the job you expect.

MORAL:

Give your customers a "promised by" date that gives you more than enough time to produce quality work...giving you the opportunity to deliver sooner, and thrilling your customer!

BE QUICK, BUT DON'T SACRIFICE QUALITY!

49

DO ACCEPT CHECKS

Ever walk into an establishment and the first thing you see is a sign reading, "Sorry, NO Checks"? That's not the way to win customers! It may offend some customers and others who want to make a purchase, will decide it's easier to go elsewhere to make their purchase rather than try to find an ATM machine. Don't be afraid to accept checks because of the loss you may incur. If you calculate it correctly, the percentage of bounced checks should be included in the cost of doing business, same as the credit card charges.

WHY IS THAT?

One day I was so mad that a $50 check bounced, I asked one of my employees to post a "NO Checks sign". Two weeks later, a customer, who owns the pool shop in the mall across the street, walked

in and told me that was a big mistake. I explained about the bouncing check. He told me he took checks and didn't even ask for driver's licenses...and rarely did he get a check that bounced. I replied that if his customers need pool supplies, they were all rich!! He said that was not the issue. The issue is one of trust and calculating the cost of keeping good, honest customers. He was 100% right!

MORAL:

Learn to trust your customers and your business will reap the rewards.

TRUST YOUR CUSTOMERS AND
THEY'LL BE BACK!

50

DO ACCEPT CREDIT CARDS

It is a must that entrepreneurs accept credit cards. Sure there is a small fee for you, however, the advantages far outweigh the disadvantages. America is a country built on debt. Just look at the national debt! The average American doesn't even carry cash anymore. They carry plastic because it's easier to keep track of their expenses, replaceable if lost, and more convenient for the consumers. I would like to emphasize that you should even accept American Express. Lots of companies don't because it costs more for them, or American Express did not authorize them for one reason or another. If you can be authorized to accept American Express...do it. It sets a better image for your company and other businesses who deal with you.

WHY IS THAT?

I find that people or customers who carry American Express tend to spend more! So don't hesitate...accept all major credit cards. You never know when that big purchaser will call or come in carrying only a credit card. Do you really want to inform that customer, "Sorry, I don't accept America Express (or whatever card)"; then watch that customer walk over to your competitor's to make his purchase? Don't shoot yourself...just accept plastic!

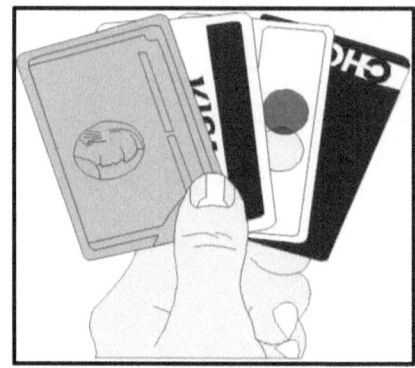

MORAL:

People spend more using their credit cards than writing checks or using cash. Don't give them the opportunity to walk out. Accept credit cards!

LET THEM CHARGE IT...
IT'S THE AMERICAN WAY!

51

DO FOLLOW YOUR MONEY

Most customers will pay for their purchases with credit cards or checks. However, if the majority of your sales are business to business, you may find it necessary to bill your clients on a monthly basis. Welcome headache and hassle! First of all, check all credit references before you open up their account. Also stay on top of all the account receivables (AR). Have a set procedure on how to collect. Whether it be a monthly bill, followed by a telephone call, followed by a collection company or something else. A system needs to be in place. You MUST keep your eyes on your money! Don't let your collections get behind.

WHY IS THAT?

The longer it takes people/businesses to

pay you, the better the odds are of not collecting the money at all!

MORAL:

Follow your money. COLLECT IT AS SOON AS POSSIBLE!

SET UP A COLLECTION SYSTEM
AND STICK TO IT!

52

DON'T EXTEND CREDIT TO LITTLE CUSTOMERS

I don't mean small people when I say little customers. I'm referring here to customers who don't spend much money on your product or service. No matter what kind of business you are in, some customers will want to open up an account so they can come in at any time and charge all their purchases from you. That is fine, if they meet the account qualifications you've established. You should set minimum as well as maximum guidelines. A minimum guideline is the minimum amount needed to be spent every month in order to qualify customers to be able to open a charge account. If you don't have minimum guidelines, it's too easy for those customers to never pay you or simply disappear.

WHY IS THAT?

In my copy center, I had a customer who came twice a month to make copies and, foolishly, I approved his account because he told me he would give me a lot of business. My staff bent over backwards to make him a satisfied customer. However, he continued to only charge about $30 a month. It cost me more than to do his monthly billing. One day he just disappeared. He was not worth extending credit to.

MORAL:

For customers who want to open an account, but spend only a small amount for your product or service, advise them you will gladly accept their credit cards. If they don't have a credit card....tough luck. You are in business to make money, not give charity.

SET ACCOUNT GUIDELINES AND STICK TO THEM!

"The Dawn Does Not Come Twice To Awaken A Man."

Arabic proverb

TIME TO SELL

WHAT TO DO AND WHAT NOT TO DO TO DETERMINE IF IT'S TIME TO SELL

53

DON'T BE AFRAID OF GOLIATH

An entrepreneur should be like David who was young and smart. Be young in your heart and smart in your mind! What makes you different from everyone else in similar businesses? Find your niche in the marketplace. Study the following:

What does the "Goliath" have and what kind of service do they provide?

What is the level of your customer loyalty?

Where are your prices compared to Goliath's?

If your prices are higher, does your service compensate for them?

Visit Goliath. Study Goliath.

What product or service could YOU specialize in that will set you apart from Goliath?

Remember, service is an asset you can count on.

WHY IS THAT?

If you think Goliath is coming to your town, you have to do some planning, decide upon your niche, and focus directly on that. You may feel like running out of town, but that is an option of being a chicken.

Moral:

If you've got it (a niche), flaunt it!

FIND YOUR NICHE!

54

DO PLAN FOR GOLIATH

It a matter of the big shark eating the small one. All a part of life. Only the fittest survive. I don't feel sorry for the small bookstore owner who was very successful, until one day when Berne's and Noble (Goliath) opened up next door and began stealing his customers. The bookstore owner had been so busy that he neglected to plan ahead, to plan for expansion while retaining customers. If you are planning to start such a business, you need to be aware of the big guy...because he will come. You need to be prepared and start fighting him before he even arrives!

WHY IS THAT?

Why should you plan for Goliath? Because if you don't plan for a way to keep your customers through great service, a great product, a great satisfaction

guarantee, a great effort on your part of going the extra mile for them, when Goliath moves in next door with lower prices, you will lose your customers and be forced to close up shop. Customer Loyalty is a thing of the past. Customers are very fickle these days. Their loyalty, if they have any, is very short lived....unless you do something about it!.

MORAL:

Keep on keeping your customers happy.

GO THE EXTRA MILE FOR YOUR CUSTOMERS!

55

DO KNOW WHEN TO FOLD

"The Gambler", sung by Kenny Rogers is a great song, but more importantly, it holds a message every entrepreneur should take to heart. Know when to fold and walk away. Every entrepreneur should sing this song once in a while. Every time you attempt to make money on your own, you are in business for yourself. You are an entrepreneur. Your are smart, first of all, for being a risk taker. But just as smart, is knowing when to fold.

WHY IS THAT?

Entrepreneurs tend to love what they're doing. They become so emotionally involved they just aren't looking at the big picture anymore or simply just can't let go. They forget that they are running a business, not nurturing a child. Therefore, do not forget to understand the value of this section.

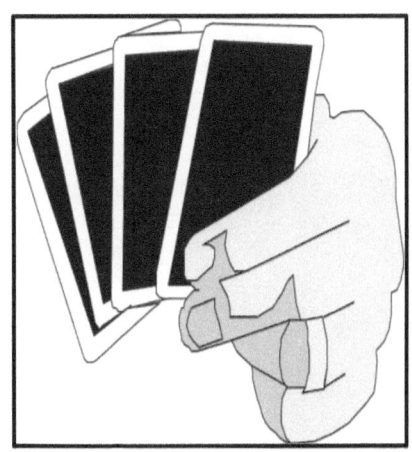

MORAL:

You must know when it's time to walk away in order to keep your profits and reduce your losses.

EVERYTHING HAS ITS SEASON...
KNOW WHEN IT'S TIME TO CLOSE UP SHOP!

56

DO SELL WHEN YOU GET AN OFFER

When I say sell, I mean sell. If you get an offer to sell your business, do it. Your age should NOT stop you. You'd be amazed at the opportunities that will open up to you, after you sell, that did not exist or you did not pay attention to because you were so involved in building and keeping your business. So go ahead...sell....and enjoy!

WHY IS THAT?

You are an entrepreneur, you get your biggest joy from starting something and watching it grow. When it's grown, it's time to sell and move on to bigger and better things!

MORAL:

Keep joy in your life. As an entrepreneur that's through exploring the unknown by creating and growing new businesses. You can't do that when you're involved in a mature business.

SELL IF YOU RECEIVE A REASONABLE OFFER!

SUMMARY

DO'S AND DON'TS
OF
DOING BUSINESS

THE DO'S AND DON'TS OF DOING BUSINESS

The Start-Up
Do think big
Do be positive
Don't associate with negative-minded people
Do get into a business you like and enjoy
Don't get into a business you have no knowledge about
Don't start from scratch
Do buy an established business
Don't buy a losing company
Don't join a franchise
Don't get into retail if you don't like dealing with people
Do believe in your product
Do have a short-term plan
Do have a long-term plan
Do secure your idea
Do incorporate
Don't use your own money
Don't borrow from relatives
Do have working capital
Don't buy expensive equipment
Don't buy second-hand from people you don't trust
Don't sign expensive leases
Don't sign long-term leases
Do pay COD when you start

Conducting Business
Do select a nice color logo
Do look clean
Don't become a cheap employee
Don't let the business own you
Do stay healthy: physically and mentally
Don't hire relatives
Don't hire close friends
Do hire people with nice smiles
Do hire good-looking people
Do hire people smarter than you
Do hire outside sales people

Do give incentives to boost morale
Do listen to your employees' advice
Do advertise
Do have annual promotions and sales

The Customer
Do know your customer type (target market)
Do kiss ass with your customers
Do listen, listen, and listen
Do know what your customers expect
Do make customer satisfaction your number one priority
Do deliver more than customers expect
Do have on-time service
Do have quick service
Do accept checks
Do accept credit cards
Do follow your money
Don't extend credit to little customers

Time to Sell?
Don't be afraid of Goliath
Do plan for Goliath
Do know when to fold
Do sell when you get an offer

SUGGESTIONS / COMMENTS

As one entrepreneur to another, we welcome your suggestions and comments about this manual. If you have any personal stories you'd like to share, or ideas for subjects not covered in this manual that you believe should be, please complete below and mail to:

Samir Hanna Safar

13790 Rosecroft Way

San Diego, CA 92130

If we use your suggestions, comments, or story in following volumes of *The 56 Small Business Rules*, we will buy the copyright for ten dollars ($10.00).